50 Weight Loss Juices:

Look Thinner in 10 Days or Less!

By

Joseph Correa

Certified Sports Nutritionist

COPYRIGHT

© 2016 Finibi Inc

All rights reserved

Reproduction or translation of any part of this work beyond that permitted by section 107 or 108 of the 1976 United States Copyright Act without the permission of the copyright owner is unlawful.

This publication is designed to provide accurate and authoritative information in regard to the subject matter covered. It is sold with the understanding that neither the author nor the publisher is engaged in rendering medical advice. If medical advice or assistance is needed, consult with a doctor. This book is considered a guide and should not be used in any way detrimental to your health. Consult with a physician before starting this nutritional plan to make sure it's right for you.

ACKNOWLEDGEMENTS

The realization and success of this book could not have been possible without the motivation and support of my entire family.

50 Weight Loss Juices:

Look Thinner in 10 Days or Less!

By

Joseph Correa

Certified Sports Nutritionist

CONTENTS

Copyright

Acknowledgements

About The Author

Introduction

50 Weight Loss Juices: Look Thinner in 10 Days or Less!

Other Great Titles by This Author

ABOUT THE AUTHOR

As a certified sports nutritionist, I honestly believe in the positive effects that proper nutrition can have over the body and mind. My knowledge and experience has helped me live healthier throughout the years and which I have shared with family and friends. The more you know about eating and drinking healthier, the sooner you will want to change your life and eating habits.

Nutrition is a key part in the process of being healthy and living longer so get started today.

INTRODUCTION

50 Weight Loss Juices will help you lose weight naturally and efficiently. These are not to replace meals but should complement your normal day to day meals.

Being too busy to eat right can sometimes become a problem and that's why this book will save you time and help nourish your body to achieve the goals you want.

This book will help you to:

-Lose weight fast.

-Reduce Fat.

-Have more energy.

-Naturally accelerate Your Metabolism to become thinner.

-Improve your digestive system.

Joseph Correa is a certified sports nutritionist and a professional athlete.

50 WEIGHT LOSS JUICES

1. Apple Mix Juice

This is a great juice to have before exercise or after dinner, and it is a great way of helping you with your weight loss. And why is that? Apples are low in calories and their fiber helps you feel fuller for a longer time, because it expands the stomach, which means fewer calories in your stomach. Cucumber juice is very rich in water, and you know that water is important for weight loss. In a recent study, adults consuming extra water lost 4 pounds of body weight more than those who did not. Apple: Improves neurological health

- Cucumber: Aids in weight loss and digestion
- Lemon: Helps in reducing pain and inflammation in joints and knees
- Orange: Regulates high blood pressure
- Banana: Plays a role in preserving memory and boosts your mood

Ingredients:

- Apple - 1 medium 162g

- Cucumber - 1 cucumber (301g
- Lemon - 1/2 fruit 25g
- Orange - 1 large 154g
- Banana- 1 medium 150 g

How to prepare:

- **Wash all the ingredients. Peel if necessary.**
- **Juice them all together for a great drink.**

Total amount of calories: 280

Vitamins: Vitamin A 27µg, Vitamin C 101.2mg, Calcium 108mg, Vitamin B-6 0.328mg, Vitamin E 1.54mg, Vitamin K 49.7µg

Minerals: Copper 0.418mg, Magnesium 52mg, Phosphorus 137mg, Selenium 2.1µg, Zinc 1.07mg

2. Fruit Mania Juice

Taste this awesome juice that is not only delightful but is also going to help you lose weight faster and cleanse your body. Ingredients like cayenne pepper may help stoke your metabolic fire. Mango, "the fruit of India", as it is sometimes called, has a wealth of nutrients, and it is a superior source of beta-carotene and vitamin C. That means, the more nutrients you get, the less you have to eat per meal. So make sure to add this juice to your daily meals.

- Apple: Protects the body from free radicals effects
- Cayenne Pepper: Possible anti-cancer agent
- Mango: Improves digestion
- Orange: Alkalizes the body
- Banana: Lowers blood pressure

Ingredients:

- Apple – 1 large 213g
- Cayenne Pepper (spice) - 1 pinch 0.11g
- Mango (peeled) - 1 fruit (without grain) 316g
- Orange (peeled) - 1 large 154g

- Banana (peeled) – 1 medium 150 g

How to prepare:

- **Wash all the ingredients. Peel if necessary.**
- **Juice them all together for a great drink.**

Total calories: 265

Vitamins: Vitamin A 128µg, Vitamin C 122.1mg, Vitamin B-6 0.409mg, Vitamin E 2.38mg, Vitamin K 12.1µg, Calcium 68mg, Iron 0.72mg

Minerals: Copper 0.319mg, Magnesium 41mg, Phosphorus 68mg, Selenium 1.9µg, Zinc 0.31mg

3. Apple Magic Juice

This is another delicious juice that will help you improve your lifestyle, and accelerate the rate at which you lose weight. Carrots fight fat because of their fiber content, more than half is soluble fiber calcium pectate. This helps lower blood-cholesterol levels by eliminating bile acids. In the end, cholesterol will be drawn out of the bloodstream to make more bile acids, and this will lower your cholesterol. It also helps eliminate excess fluids from the body. Enjoy this juice and include it in your daily routine. It will give you positive results.

- Apples : Prevent dementia
- Carrots: Prevent stroke
- Ginger Root: Helps control the heart rate
- Lemon: Prevents growth and multiplication of pathogenic bacteria
- Mango: Helps in diabetes

Ingredients:

- Apples - 1 medium 180g
- Carrots - 2 medium 112g
- Ginger Root - 1/2 thumb 10g

- Lemon (peeled) - 1/2 fruit 25g
- Mango (peeled) – 1/2 fruit 70 g

How to prepare:

- **Wash all the ingredients. Peel if necessary.**
- **Juice them all together for a great drink.**

Total calories: 161

Vitamins: Vitamin A 521µg, Vitamin C 17.9mg, Calcium 30mg, Iron 0.53mg, Vitamin B-6 0.212mg, Vitamin E 1.02mg, Vitamin K 12.9µg

Minerals: Copper 0.114mg, Magnesium 21mg, Phosphorus 54mg, Selenium 0.1µg, Zinc 0.25mg

4. Weight Loss Booster Juice

Here is a simple juice recipe, yet very effective for weight loss. Cabbage is not consumed as much as it should be. It's a great source of vitamin C, and has a high content of fiber. Pears are also a good source of fiber. Studies have shown that if you eat more than three pears a day, you will consume fewer calories and you will lose more weight. They also have a really high level of fructose and glucose; this provides a natural source of energy. Pears contain boron and this helps the body to retain calcium, making you healthier. It's a great recipe for you and your family.

- Apple: Reduces the risk of diabetes
- Cabbage: Helps lowering blood pressure
- Lemon: Helps cure the common cold
- Pears: Prevent cancer

Ingredients:

- Apple- 1 medium 180 g
- Cabbage (red) - 3 leaves 72g
- Lemon (with rind) - 1/2 fruit 27g
- Pears - 2 medium 346g

How to prepare:

- **Wash all the ingredients. Peel if necessary.**
- **Juice them all together for a great drink.**

Total calories: 205

Vitamins: Vitamin A 29µg, Vitamin C 48.1mg, Thiamin 0.059mg, Vitamin B-6 0.213mg, Vitamin E 0.3mg, Vitamin K 33.6µg, Calcium 52mg

Minerals: Copper 0.203mg, Magnesium 27mg, Phosphorus 50mg, Selenium 0.6µg, Zinc 0.3mg

5. Super Spinach Juice

Spinach is a great source of fiber for our digestive system. It is a cleansing agent which removes waste that has accumulated over time in the digestive tracts. Because of its laxative effect on the body, it will also improve the tracts functions.Lemon has always been a great ingredient when trying to lose weight, as well as apples, since they help lower your cholesterol. It's a delicious juice that you can enjoy at any time.

- Celery: It helps you calm down
- Lemon: Aids in the production of digestive juices
- Pears: Help in building up your immune system
- Orange: Regulates High Blood Pressure
- Spinach: Keeps the skin and hair healthy
- Apples: Lower bad cholesterol

Ingredients:

- Celery – 3 stalks, large 206g
- Lemon (peeled) – ½ fruit 25g
- Pear- 1 medium 170g
- Orange (peeled) – 1 large 180g

- Spinach – 4 handful 100g

- Apples – 2 medium 350g

How to prepare:

- **Wash all the ingredients. Peel if necessary.**

- **Juice them all together for a great drink.**

Total calories: 243

Vitamins: Vitamin A 406µg, Vitamin C 107.2mg, Calcium 219mg, Iron 3.16mg, Choline 45.9mg, Vitamin B-6 0.56mg, Vitamin K 413.5µg

Minerals: Copper 0.253mg, Magnesium 114mg, Phosphorus 121mg, Selenium 1.3µg, Zinc 0.67mg

6. Wonderful Fresh Juice

If losing weight is your goal, try this juice recipe. It will push you in the right direction. Beets are a great way to cleanse the blood, and strengthen the gall bladder and liver. Carrots help the liver to cleanse and to release more bile, and at the same time will boost your immune system, giving you a healthy body. They also contain beta-carotene which is known for reducing the risk of several cancers. The nutrients contained in this juice will provide you with a lot of fiber, and can easily replace a meal if necessary, but with the advantage of having fewer calories. This is a delicious recipe you should add in your daily life.

- Beetroot: Detoxification support
- Banana: Reduces risk of leukemia
- Carrots: Improve vision
- Pepper: Migraine headache prevention

Ingredients:

- Beetroot - 1/2 beet 40g
- Banana – 1 medium 150g
- Carrots - 3 large 206g

- Pepper (sweet red) - 1/2 medium 54g

How to prepare:

- **Wash all the ingredients. Peel if necessary.**
- **Juice them all together for a great drink.**

Total calories: 85

Vitamins: Vitamin A 1128µg, Vitamin C 59.5mg, Calcium 51mg, Choline 13.4mg, Folate 61µg, Vitamin B-6 0.319mg, Vitamin E 1.27mg

Minerals: Copper 0.047mg, Magnesium 25mg, Phosphorus 65mg, Selenium 0.3µg, Zinc 0.46mg

7. Fountain of life

Here is a healthy and appetizing juice recipe that will help you in losing weight. Beets are very useful in helping the liver to cleanse, that means the liver will help metabolize fat more effectively. The liver will get an additional boost from carrots, as they have powerful properties which will detoxify it. They also eliminate excess fluids that lay in the body. Oranges have about 59 calories per fruit; they are fat-free, and high in fiber. They really help to drop those extra pounds. Only good results can come from drinking this juice.

- Apple: Powerful natural antioxidant
- Beetroot: Fights inflammation
- Carrots: Reduce risk of lung cancer
- Parsley: Excellent blood purifier
- Orange: Provides smart carbs

Ingredients:

- Apple - 1 medium 180g
- Beetroot - 1/2 beet 40g
- Carrots - 3 medium 170g
- Parsley - 1 handful 40g

- Orange (peeled) - 1 medium 140 g

How to prepare:

- **Wash all the ingredients. Peel if necessary.**

- **Juice them all together for a great drink.**

Total calories: 110

Vitamins: Vitamin A 1012µg, Vitamin C 34.8mg, Calcium 109mg, Iron 2.38mg, Vitamin B-6 0.14mg, Vitamin E 1.24mg, Vitamin K 305.2µg

Minerals: Copper 0.127mg, Magnesium 32mg, Phosphorus 88mg, Selenium 0.4µg, Zinc 0.67m

8. Banana Max Juice

Let's see if this delicious juice fits your needs. The great thing about juices is they give you all the nutrients you need. The idea is you eat less and have fewer junk food craving. Celery has high calcium content, and helps controlling high blood pressure. Let's not forget that ginger helps digesting fatty foods, and adding lemon juice to any beverage will help accelerate weight loss. Enjoy this juice whenever you want. It can easily replace any snack.

- Banana: Supports heart health
- Cabbage: High in sulfur, the beautifying mineral
- Celery: Contains good salts
- Cider Vinegar: Kills pathogens, including bacteria
- Ginger root: Controls blood pressure
- Grapes: Reduce risk of cancer

Ingredients:

- Banana (peeled) – 1 medium 150g
- Cabbage (red) – ¼ head, medium 201 g
- Celery – 2stalks, 142g

- Cider Vinegar (apple) – 1 tbsp 14.9g

- Ginger Root – 1 thumb 24g

- Grapes – 14 grapes 80g

How to prepare:

- **Wash all the ingredients. Peel if necessary.**

- **Juice them all together for a great drink.**

Total calories: 130

Vitamins: Vitamin A 108μg, Vitamin C 98mg, Vitamin B-6 0.429mg, Vitamin E 0.64mg, Vitamin K 74.3μg, Niacin 1.202mg, Calcium 142mg

Minerals: Copper 0.211mg, Magnesium 54mg, Phosphorus 107mg, Selenium 1.2μg, Zinc 0.4mg

9. Cooler Juice

Our modern lifestyle makes us take the wrong decisions many times when it comes to diet. Here is a juice recipe that takes just a few minutes to prepare, and it will give you a healthy start to your day. Peaches are low on calories, so they can help you stick to a reduced calorie diet. Basil seeds are a great source of fiber, and they have a reputation for their weight loss benefits. Basil: Reduces inflammation and swelling

- Carrots: Are a powerful antiseptic

- Peaches: Lower risk of cancer

- Apple: Protects neuron cells against oxidative stress

Ingredients:

- Basil (fresh) - 3 leaves 1.5g

- Carrots - 14 medium 854g

- Peaches - 5 medium   750g

- Apple -1 medium 180 g

How to prepare:

- **Wash all the ingredients. Peel if necessary.**

- **Juice them all together for a great drink.**

Total calories: 352

Vitamins: Vitamin A 4079µg, Vitamin C 75mg, Calcium 208mg, Vitamin B-6 0.911mg, Vitamin E 5.83mg, Vitamin K 76.9µg, Choline 56.2mg

Minerals: Copper 0.621mg, Magnesium 102mg, Phosphorus 290mg, Selenium 1.1µg, Zinc 2.25mg

10. Fruit Express Juice

This is a great juice that will help you drop pounds or kilos and increase your energy. The ingredients used in this recipe will help you with your digestion, stimulating the digestive juices, and will lower your cholesterol. If you consume two apples per day, it lowers your cholesterol by as much as 17 percent, so that says a lot. Let's not forget to mention that it's full of nutrients, and the calories consumed are quite low. So you get the same result as a meal, but actually you consume fewer calories. It's definitely ideal for weight loss.

- Apples: Reduce risk of thrombotic stroke
- Carrots: Cleanse the body
- Lemon: Strengthens the liver
- Peaches: Support hearth health
- Banana: Lower blood pressure

Ingredients:

- Apples - 1 large 200g
- Carrots – 8 medium 500g
- Lemon (outer skin cut off) - 1/2 fruit 40g
- Peaches - 2 large 300g

- Banana (peeled) - 1 medium 150g

How to prepare:

- **Wash all the ingredients. Peel if necessary.**
- **Juice them all together for a great drink.**

Total calories: 410

Vitamins: Vitamin A 3128μg, Vitamin C 109.8mg, Calcium 194mg, Vitamin B-6 0.819mg, Vitamin E 4.44mg, Vitamin K 54.3μg, Choline 55.7mg

Minerals: Copper 0.412mg, Magnesium 94mg, Phosphorus 206mg, Selenium 1.2μg, Zinc 1.37mg

11. Gold Juice

This is the perfect juice for you if you are looking for something to help you have a smaller waist line. One of the benefits of using kale is that it provides a large nutritional punch with fewer calorie counts per cup. Celery helps to calm nervousness because it has high calcium content and will help in controlling blood pressure. It also lowers cholesterol levels because of the pectin that can be found in apples, so this juice can turn into a real friend while losing weight.

- Apple: Reduces the risk of developing cancer, diabetes, and heart disease.

- Celery: Delivers up to 10 percent of your daily need for Vitamin A

- Cucumber: Helps prevent diabetes, reduces cholesterol, and controls blood pressure.

- Ginger root: Very effective in alleviating symptoms of gastrointestinal distress

- Kale: Is a great anti-inflammatory food

- Lemon: Helps maintain your immune system

Ingredients:

- Apples - 2 medium   364g

- Celery - 2 stalks, 128g

- Cucumber - 1 cucumber 290g

- Ginger Root - 1 thumb 20g

- Kale - 4 leaves (8-12") 120g

- Lemon - 1/2 fruit 40g

How to prepare:

- **Wash all the ingredients. Peel if necessary.**

- **Juice them all together for a great drink.**

Total calories: 215

Vitamins: Vitamin B-6 0.77mg, Vitamin E 1.09mg, Niacin 2.637mg, Thiamin 0.315mg, Vitamin K 1128.7µg

Minerals: Copper 2.47mg, Magnesium 119mg, Phosphorus 207mg, Zinc 1.65mg

12. Energizer Juice

If you were looking for a juice that will help you with your diet or weight loss, you should consider this one. Beets are a great way for purifying not only the blood, but also your liver, and that is a great thing because it helps metabolize fat, so you get rid of it faster. Carrots help you to eliminate excess fluids from the body, so water retention is reduced, especially for women. You will get an energy boost because of the high content in fiber, and it will be a healthy way to fuel your body.

- Beetroot: great to boost your stamina

- Cabbage: Full of vitamin K, helps with mental function and concentration

- Carrots: Prevent heart disease

- Lemon: Plays the role of blood purifier

- Orange: Protects skin

- Pineapple: Prevents asthma

- Spinach: One of the best sources of dietary potassium

Ingredients:

- Beetroot - 1 beet 155g

- Cabbage (red) - 2 leaves 40g

- Carrots - 2 medium 143g

- Lemon - 1/2 fruit 40g

- Orange - 1 fruit 121g

- Pineapple - 1/3 fruit 206g

- Spinach - 2 handful 50g

How to prepare:

- **Wash all the ingredients. Peel if necessary.**

- **Juice them all together for a great drink.**

Total calories: 195

Vitamins: Vitamin B-6 0.60mg, Vitamin E 1.58mg, Vitamin K 149.6µg, Choline 43.8mg, Folate 261µg, Niacin 2.136mg

Minerals: **Copper 0.317mg, Magnesium 97mg, Phosphorus 131mg, Selenium 2.1µg, Zinc 1.22mg**

13. Refresh Juice

Beets help detoxify the body, so this juice is perfect for a weight loss program. Drinking lemon juice helps in relaxing the mind and body by reducing stress. Carrots do an awesome job in increasing the production of your white blood cells, and that helps you build a stronger immune system, which leads in the end to a stronger body.

- Apples: Are extremely rich in important antioxidants
- Beetroot: Has anti –cancer effects
- Carrots: High level of beta-carotene acts as an antioxidant to prevent cell damage
- Lemon: Aids the production of digestive juices
- Orange: Fights against viral infections

Ingredients:

- Apple – 1 medium 152g
- Beetroot – 1 beet 165g
- Carrots – 10 medium 560g
- Lemon – ½ fruit 40g
- Oranges (peeled) – 2 fruits 242g

How to prepare:

- **Wash all the ingredients. Peel if necessary.**
- **Juice them all together for a great drink.**

Total calories: 275

Vitamins: Vitamin B-6 0.945mg, Vitamin E 4.01mg, Vitamin K 60.8μg, Choline 71.4mg, Folate 233μg, Niacin 5.101mg

Minerals: Copper 0.40mg, Magnesium 107mg, Phosphorus 243mg, Selenium 2.3μg, Zinc 1.81mg

14. Lemon Taste Juice

Adding lemon juice to a beverage will help increase weight loss. This juice recipe is great for a weight loss diet. Lemons help controlling high blood pressure and are also a great source of Vitamin C. It is best served after dinner and combined with an active lifestyle. All of these ingredients will help you lower your cholesterol, and will resolve all your indigestion problems.

- Blueberry: Neutralizes free radicals which might cause disease and aging

- Lemon: Helps balancing the calcium and oxygen levels in the liver

- Pomegranate: Regenerates cell

Ingredients:

- Blueberry - 1 cup 128g

- Lemon - 1/4 fruit 20g

- Pomegranate - 1 pomegranate (262g

How to prepare;

- **Wash all the ingredients.**

- **The pomegranate can be added with the membrane attached, you save some time, and the taste will still be great.**

- **Juice them all together for a great drink.**

Total calories: 168

Vitamins: Vitamin A 3µg, Vitamin C 27mg, Vitamin B-6 0.209mg, Vitamin E 1.6mg, Vitamin K 49.4µg, Choline 21mg, Folate 63µg

Minerals: Copper 0.346mg, Magnesium 28mg, Phosphorus 76mg, Selenium 1.2µg, Zinc 0.57mg

15. Feel Alive Juice

This is a wonderful juice for those of you who like peppermint. Ginger plays a big role in lowering LDL cholesterol, because the spice in it reduces the entire amount of cholesterol that gets absorbed. It also helps with the digestion of fatty foods and breaking down proteins. Oranges have an alkaline effect in the digestive system that stimulates digestive juices, so you get a more active metabolism. Give it a try. It will help you get rid of those hard to lose kilograms or pounds.

- Fennel Bulb: Has good levels of heart-friendly electrolyte potassium
- Ginger Root: Contains health benefiting essential oils
- Lemon: It balances and maintains the pH levels in the body
- Orange: Reduces risk of liver cancer
- Peppermint: Inhibits growth of prostate cancer

Ingredients:

- Fennel Bulb (whole with fronds) - 1 bulb 200g
- Ginger Root - 1/2 thumb 14g
- Lemon - 1/2 fruit 25g

- Orange (peeled) - 1 large 160g
- Peppermint - 5 leaves 0.25g

How to prepare:

- **Wash all the ingredients. Peel if necessary.**
- **Juice them all together for a great drink.**

Total calories: 84

Vitamins: Vitamin A 14µg, Vitamin C 79.4mg, Vitamin B-6 0.144mg, Folate 66µg, Niacin 1.358mg, Riboflavin 0.101mg

Minerals: Copper 0.173mg, Magnesium 36mg, Phosphorus 96mg, Selenium 2mg, Zinc 0.41mg

16. Apple Heart Juice

This juice will help you get healthier and lose weight at the same time. Nutrients from juices are easily absorbed by our bodies and that will equate to a faster metabolism. Apples help you lower your cholesterol because of the pectin they contain. Lemons are always great when trying to drop the fat in your body. Just think of this juice as a friend who wants to help you lose some weight.

- Apple: Prevents breast cancer

- Cranberries: Reduce risk of cardiovascular disease

- Ginger Root: Has anti-inflammatory effects

- Lemon: Prevents formation of wrinkles and acne

Ingredients:

- Apples - 3 medium 500g

- Cranberries - 1/2 cup 50g

- Ginger Root - 1/4 thumb 6g

- Lemon - 1/2 fruit 42g

How to prepare:

- **Wash all the ingredients. Peel if necessary.**
- **Juice them all together for a great drink.**

Total calories: 204

Vitamins: Vitamin A 23µg, Vitamin C 101.5mg, Iron 0.68mg, Vitamin B-6 0.214mg, Vitamin E 1.19mg, Vitamin K 9.2µg, Calcium 76mg

Minerals: Copper 0.193mg, Magnesium 35mg, Phosphorus 61mg, Selenium 0.7µg, Zinc 0.25mg

17. Any Time Juice

Losing fat comes as a result of drinking natural juices, and here is one recipe you will really like. Ginger's greatest benefit is that it will help you digest fatty foods and break down proteins. Spinach has high fiber content, so that helps you get more energy for lower calories. Celery is considered by many a negative-calorie food and by adding celery to your diet, you will increase your weight loss results without so much effort. Taste it, feel it, and let it help you with your daily weight loss routine.

- Apples: Reduce risk of stroke

- Celery: Aids digestion

- Cucumber: Relieves bad breath

- Ginger root: Has anti-microbial effects

- Lemon: Maintains the health of the eyes

- Lime: Excellent weight reducer

- Spinach: Cancer prevention

Ingredients:

- Apples - 2 medium 350g

- Celery - 3 stalks, large 182g

- Cucumber - 1 cucumber 300g

- Ginger Root - 1/2 thumb 10g

- Lemon (with rind) - 1/2 fruit 41g

- Lime (with rind) - 1 fruit 65g

- Spinach - 2 cups 50g

How to prepare:

- **Wash all the ingredients. Peel if necessary.**

- **Juice them all together for a great drink.**

Total calories: 185

Vitamins: Vitamin A 648µg, Vitamin C 198.9mg, Calcium 304mg, Vitamin B-6 0.422mg, Vitamin E 2.39mg, Vitamin K 1904.6µg, Niacin 2.607mg

Minerals: Copper 0.395mg, Magnesium 129mg, Phosphorus 201mg, Selenium 1.9µg, Zinc 2.04mg

18. Lemony Apple Juice

Drinking juice is a great way to get concentrated nutrients into our body. This next recipe is a great one, it helps our digestive system function better by cleansing the stomach and kidneys, and that leads ultimately to a stronger body. This juice will lower your cholesterol because of the particular ingredients it has. Watermelon juice prevents the clogging of arteries and at the same time increases the HDL, which is the good cholesterol. This is a great juice to have before any exercise routine, it is an excellent source of energy.

- Lemon: Aids in production of digestive juices
- Tomato: Maintains blood pressure
- Watermelon: Prevents asthma
- Apple: Improves neurological health

Ingredients:

- Lemon - 1/2 fruit 40g
- Tomato - 1 large whole 171g
- Watermelon - 1 large wedge 560g
- Apple – 1 medium 175g

How to prepare:

- **Wash all the ingredients. Peel if necessary.**

- **Juice them all together for a great drink.**

Total calories: 135

Vitamins: Vitamin A 176µg, Vitamin C 68.5mg, Vitamin B-6 0.326mg, Vitamin E 0.98mg, Vitamin K 11.5µg, Calcium 58mg, Iron 1.70mg

Minerals: Copper 0.264mg, Magnesium 57mg, Phosphorus 69mg, Selenium 1.6µg, Zinc 0.61mg

19. Green Power Juice

Juices are a great way of keeping our body healthy and help us get in shape. Every time you mash up foods like vegetables or fruits, they become incredibly easier to absorb. It means all the vital nutrients will be absorbed into the body at a faster rate than vitamins or other supplements. Carrots eliminate excess fluids from the body, and because of vitamin A and Beta-carotene, carrots may reduce the risk of several cancers. It's a great way to protect and nourish your body with just one drink.

- Apple: Lowers levels of bad cholesterol
- Cabbage: Helps detoxify the body
- Carrots: Prevent heart disease
- Ginger Root: Contains health benefiting essential oils
- Spinach: Contributes to bone health

Ingredients:

- Apples - 2 medium 364g
- Cabbage (red) - 1/4 head, 140g
- Carrots - 4 medium 244g
- Ginger Root - 1/2 10g

- Spinach - 4 handful 100g

How to prepare:

- **Wash all the ingredients. Peel if necessary.**
- **Juice them all together for a great drink.**

Total calories: 200

Vitamins: Vitamin A 1818µg, Vitamin C 120mg, Vitamin B-6 0.73mg, Vitamin E 3.2mg, Vitamin K 404.1µg, Calcium 198mg, Niacin 2.936mg

Minerals: Copper 0.288mg, Magnesium 111mg, Phosphorus 161mg, Selenium 1.7µg, Zinc 1.15mg

20. Morning Start

People are in serious need of a healthy alternative to eating artificial and processed foods. Too many people gain weight because they can't control how much they eat. Certain protein compounds in spinach are beneficial in lowering high blood pressure. The pectin in apples, pears and carrots lowers cholesterol levels as well. Ginger increases blood circulation, and because of this great mixture, you get a high amount of fructose and glucose, making sure you have the necessary energy for an active day. This juice can be enjoyed in the morning or after dinner; it is a super drink when trying to eat higher quality food contents.

- Apple: Reduces the risk of diabetes

- Carrots: Maintain a healthy glowing skin

- Cucumber: Reduces cholesterol and controls blood pressure

- Ginger Root: Helps improve the intestinal motility

- Pear: Beneficial for your colon health

- Spinach: Prevents constipation and promote a healthy digestive tract

Ingredients:

- Apple - 1 medium 180g
- Carrots - 5 medium 300g
- Cucumber - 1 cucumber 300g
- Ginger Root - 1 thumb 24g
- Pear - 1 medium 165g
- Spinach - 2 handful 50g

How to prepare:

- **Wash all the ingredients. Peel if necessary.**
- **Juice them all together for a great drink.**

Total calories: 211

Vitamins: Vitamin A 1863µg, Vitamin C 60.9mg, Vitamin B-6 0.545mg, Vitamin E 2.37mg, Vitamin K 220.1µg, Calcium 151mg, Iron 2.8mg

Minerals: Copper 0.408mg, Magnesium 104mg, Phosphorus 164mg, Selenium 1.2µg, Zinc 1.28mg

21. Simply Celery

Juicing is really the art of extracting the liquid and nutrients from any fruit or vegetable. It helps create energy and vitality like few pills can achieve. This recipe will improve the rate at which you lose weight, and at the same time give you all the daily vitamins and minerals your body needs. The human body is about 75% water, so for proper bodily function, digestion and detoxification, the recommended daily intake is around 2.5 liters. Water is a strong element when trying to drop weight, so you have to concentrate on drinking a lot of it. By having this juice, you get a concentrated portion of the daily liquid requirements that your body needs, with nutrients and fiber that will provide you with a high boost of energy throughout the day.

- Apples: Reduce risk of diabetes
- Celery: Reduces inflammation
- Tangerine: Heals cuts, wounds

Ingredients:

- Apples - 2 large 440g
- Celery - 8 stalks, large 510g
- Tangerine (peeled) - 1 small 76g

How to prepare:

- **Wash all the ingredients. Peel if necessary.**
- **Juice them all together for a great drink.**

Total calories: 180

Vitamins: Vitamin A 101µg, Vitamin C 57.2mg, Calcium 162mg, Vitamin B-6 0.427mg, Vitamin E 1.5mg, Vitamin K 101.7µg, Choline 30mg

Minerals: Copper 0.217mg, Magnesium 61mg, Phosphorus 127mg, Selenium 1.3µg, Zinc 0.45mg

22. Full of Energy

This juice has a high concentration of potassium and phosphorous, which are necessary for normal body function. Tomato juice serves as a great antioxidant and will also improve digestive function. The high content of vitamin C in this juice will help in maintaining the structural integrity of bones. Onion is great to use in any recipe, because it has a low-calorie/high fiber ratio which is exactly what you need when reducing fat in the body.

- Cucumber: Fights cancers
- Onion : Scavenges free radicals
- Parsley : Great immunity booster
- Pepper : Helps relieve allergies
- Tomatoes: Reduces risk of prostate cancer

Ingredients:

- Cucumber - 1 cucumber 300g
- Onion (spring/scallion) - 1 medium 15g
- Parsley - 1 handful 40g
- Pepper (sweet red) - 1/2 medium 55g
- Tomatoes - 2 small whole 180g

How to prepare:

- **Wash all the ingredients. Peel if necessary.**
- **Juice them all together for a great drink.**

Total calories: 68

Vitamins: Vitamin A 260μg, Vitamin C 126mg, Calcium 102mg, Vitamin B-6 0.412mg, Vitamin E 2.06mg, Vitamin K 522.6μg, Calcium 90mg

Minerals: Copper 0.252mg, Magnesium 71mg, Phosphorus 114mg, Selenium 0.7μg, Zinc 1.12mg

23. Sweet Carrots

"Sweet Carrots" will help you keep your body healthy and lose weight at the same time. Bell pepper juice will significantly help in reducing cholesterol. Carrots contain beta-carotene which helps reduce the risk of cancer. The high quantity of vitamins and minerals found in this juice will definitely accelerate the rate at which you get rid of fat and start looking slimmer.

- Carrots: Replenish daily vitamins
- Celery: Aids digestion
- Cucumber: Great source of B vitamins
- Parsley: Great blood builder
- Pepper: Helps produce saliva due to cayenne
- Tomatoes: The folic acid in tomatoes can help with depression

Ingredients:

- Carrots - 2 large 144g
- Celery - 3 stalks, large 192g
- Cucumber - 1/2 cucumber 150.5g
- Parsley - 2 handful 80g

- Pepper (sweet green) - 1/2 medium 58g

- Tomatoes - 3 medium whole 360g

How to prepare:

- **Wash all the ingredients. Peel if necessary.**

- **Juice them all together for a great drink.**

Total calories: 107

Vitamins: Vitamin A 1227µg, Vitamin C 142.3mg, Vitamin B-6 0.642mg, Vitamin E 3.15mg, Vitamin K 1013.3µg, Calcium 212mg, Iron 5.55mg

Minerals: Copper 0.416mg, Magnesium 105mg, Phosphorus 200mg, Selenium 1.1µg, Zinc 1.80mg

24. Lime Delight

"Lime Delight" combines healthy natural fruits and vegetables into a single drink that will make you feel full of energy and ready for a new day. Pectin found in apples can lower your cholesterol by as much as 15 percent. Also, bell peppers help your body to increase your metabolism by lowering triglycerides, which will really make a difference when losing weight. You should consume this juice to start your day and feel the difference by the end of it.

- Apples: Help in losing weight

- Cilantro: Very rich in numerous anti- oxidants

- Cucumbers: Relieve you from bad breath

- Lime: Helps flush out toxins

- Pepper: Remedy for toothache

Ingredients:

- Apples - 2 medium 360g

- Cilantro - 1 bunch 90g

- Cucumbers - 2 cucumbers 600g

- Lime (with rind) - 1/2 fruit 30g

- Pepper (sweet green) (seeds removed) - 1/2 medium 56g

How to prepare:

- **Wash all the ingredients. Peel if necessary.**
- **Juice them all together for a great drink.**

Total calories: 179

Vitamins: Vitamin A 244µg, Vitamin C 79.2mg, Vitamin B-6 0.442mg, Vitamin E 2.1mg, Vitamin K 227.6µg, Calcium 128mg, Iron 2.68mg

Minerals: Copper 0.419mg, Magnesium 80mg, Phosphorus 153mg, Selenium 1.8µg, Zinc 1.25mg

25. Colorful Juice

I think weight loss can be a challenge for anyone who can't control how and what they eat, but with persistence and a serious mindset you can achieve anything. "Colorful Juice" will help you get closer to your goal. Asparagus contains 3 grams of fiber that will quickly cleanse the digestive system. As for celery, it helps to calm the craving for sweets, and helps in controlling high blood pressure. It contains probiotics that selectively stimulate the growth of friendly bacteria in the gut, which will aid digestion. Let's not forget to mention the high amount of nutrients that will get absorbed easier as well. This is a must drink juice if you are serious about getting in shape.

- Asparagus: Great source of nutrients
- Carrots: Vitamin A assists the liver in flushing out the toxins from the body
- Celery: Very low in calories, great choice for losing weight
- Apple: Regulates blood sugar

Ingredients:

- Asparagus - 4 spears, medium 60g

- Carrots - 3 large 216g

- Celery - 2 stalks, large 128g

- Apple – 1 medium 180g

How to prepare:

- **Wash all the ingredients. Peel if necessary.**

- **Juice them all together for a great drink.**

Total calories: 71

Vitamins: Vitamin A 1259µg, Vitamin C 14.1mg, Calcium 87mg, Iron 1.40mg, Vitamin B-6 0.302mg, Vitamin E 1.55mg, Vitamin K 61.5µg

Minerals: Copper 0.173mg, Magnesium 31mg, Phosphorus 81mg, Selenium 1.3µg, Zinc 0.61mg

26. Holiday Juice

Juicing is a fun and easy way to get fruits and veggies into your diet. This recipe is both healthy and delicious. One great benefit of adding kale into your juice is that it provides a large nutritional punch with one of the fewest calorie counts per cup in all vegetables, and that means it will help you look slimmer faster. Lemon juice helps in lowering cholesterol and gets rid of fat. You should serve this juice 30 minutes before any meal to get the most from it.

- Apples: Contain pectin and lower the LDL (bad cholesterol)
- Celery: Helps in controlling high blood pressure
- Cucumber: Contains silica, essential component of healthy connective tissue
- Ginger root: Ameliorates effects on digestive aliments
- Kale: Helps support a healthy immune system
- Lemon: Assists in curing respiratory problems
- Orange: Helps stimulate white cells to fight infection

Ingredients:

- Apples - 3 medium 540g

- Celery - 3 stalks, large 190g

- Cucumber - 1/2 cucumber 150.5g

- Ginger Root - 1/2 thumb 10g

- Kale - 4 leaves 140g

- Lemon - 1 fruit 50g

- Orange (peeled, de-seeded) - 1 large 180g

How to prepare:

- **Wash all the ingredients. Peel if necessary.**

- **Juice them all together for a great drink.**

Total calories: 295

Vitamins: Vitamin A 531µg, Vitamin C 212.8mg, Calcium 294mg, Iron 2.69mg, Vitamin B-6 0.627mg, Vitamin E 1.3mg, Vitamin K 735.8µg

Minerals: Copper 1.664mg, Magnesium 103mg, Phosphorus 211mg, Selenium 2.4µg, Zinc 1.19mg

27. Spinach Power

"Spinach Power" can replace a snack or even part of your breakfast, in the morning, if you are really hungry. It's a great source of energy and nutrients. To have a stronger body, you need all body functions to work efficiently. Beets have shown to help cleanse the blood, and help metabolize fat. Let's not forget that they are high in carbohydrates so they are a great source of energy. Celery is a great source of vitamin C and is high in fiber, which is important for the body.

- Apples: They lower risk of developing lung cancer
- Beetroot: Is a great treatment used for leukemia
- Carrots: Beta- carotene consumption reduces risk of several cancers
- Spinach: Slows down cancerous cell division, in breast cancer

Ingredients:

- Apple - 1 medium 180g
- Beetroot - 1 beet 175g
- Carrots - 8 medium 480g
- Spinach - 3 cups 90g

How to prepare:

- **Wash all the ingredients. Peel if necessary.**
- **Juice them all together for a great drink.**

Total calories: 190

Vitamins: Vitamin A 3074µg, Vitamin C 50.5mg, Calcium 218mg, Vitamin B-6 0.765mg, Vitamin E 3.05mg, Vitamin K 368.6µg, Iron 4.01mg

Minerals: Copper 0.373mg, Magnesium 125mg, Phosphorus 215mg, Selenium 2.1µg, Zinc 1.35mg

28. Health Supplier

To live better and feel great you need to stay away from junk food. This juice will supply the body with a lot of the nutrients it requires. Make this juice in the morning as a great source of energy, and it will help maintain your metabolism active for the entire day. Choline contained by beets juice is a great way to detoxify the entire digestive system. A carrot a day reduces stroke risk by 68 percent so you may think twice before skipping your vegetables. High amounts of nutrients make this juice a great way to fuel your body for the entire day accompanied by healthy food.

- Apples: May protect brain cells from the free radical damage that leads to Alzheimer.

- Beetroot: Unique source of betaine, a nutrient that helps protecting cells

- Carrots: The high level of beta-carotene acts as an antioxidant to cell damage

- Celery: It regulates the body's alkaline balance

- Ginger Root: Helps with arthritis-related problems

- Cucumber: Rehydrates the body and replenishes vitamins

Ingredients:

- Apples - 2 medium 360g
- Beetroot - 1 beet 175g
- Carrots - 4 medium 240g
- Celery - 3 stalks, 192g
- Ginger Root - 1/2 thumb 10g
- Cucumber - 1/2 cucumber 150g

How to prepare:

- **Wash all the ingredients. Peel if necessary.**
- **Juice them all together for a great drink.**

Total calories: 215

Vitamins: Vitamin A 1370µg, Vitamin C 34.2mg, Vitamin B-6 0.557mg, Vitamin E 2.04mg, Vitamin K 83.1µg, Calcium 160mg, Iron 2.40mg

Minerals: Copper 0.327mg, Magnesium 84mg, Phosphorus 167mg, Selenium 1.6µg, Zinc 1.25mg

29. Good Life

"Good Life" is vital to maintain good health and can improve your weight loss. It's easy to prepare and you get the maximum benefits when all the ingredients are fresh. Beets are great fuel for our body, containing high amounts of fiber essential to the body. Spirulina contains all the essential amino acids the body needs which will definitely be a great source when trying to get slimmer.

- Beetroot: Useful in helping cleanse the liver

- Celery: Protects the eyes and prevents age-related degeneration of vision

- Spinach: High level of iron makes it a great blood builder

- Spirulina: Increases stamina and immunity

Ingredients:

- Beetroot - 1 beet 175g

- Celery - 2 stalks, large 128g

- Spinach - 3 cups 90g

- Spirulina (dried) - 1 teaspoon 2.31g

How to prepare:

- **Wash all the ingredients. Peel if necessary.**
- **Juice them all together for a great drink.**

Total calories: 52

Vitamins: Vitamin A 308µg, Vitamin C 23.7mg, Vitamin B-6 0.257mg, Vitamin E 1.45mg, Vitamin K 311.1µg, Calcium 110mg, Iron 3.12mg

Minerals: Copper 0.291mg, Magnesium 90mg, Phosphorus 100mg, Selenium 2µg, Zinc 0.78m

30. Roll the Beet

Juices have been around for a long time and are one of the best ways to absorb all the nutrients that fruits and vegetables have to offer. "Roll the Beet" is simple to prepare and due to the low calorie intake, you will see great results soon after drinking it. The best time of the day to drink it is in the morning so you can start the day with a big boost of energy to keep you active.

- Beetroot: Lowers blood pressure in a short period of time
- Carrots: Great source of beta-carotene
- Oranges: Fight against Viral infections

Ingredients:

- Beetroot - 1 beet 170g
- Carrots - 2 medium 120g
- Oranges - 2 fruits 262g

How to prepare:

- **Wash all the ingredients. Peel if necessary.**
- **Juice them all together for a great drink.**

Total calories: 115

Vitamins: Vitamin A 726µg, Vitamin C 104.6mg, Vitamin B-6 0.29mg, Vitamin E 0.84mg, Vitamin K 11.1µg, Calcium 111mg, Iron 1.40mg

Minerals: Copper 0.211mg, Magnesium 55mg, Phosphorus 102mg, Selenium 1.7µg, Zinc 0.73mg

31. Life Punch

When you are in a rush, it's easy to be tempted to go for canned or processed foods that are out in the market simply because they are easy to attain. But easier isn't always the best way on the long term. The easy way of having a healthy daily snack that provides you with all the vitamins is juicing, and this juice is packed with vital ingredients that will improve your immune system and will fill your body with what it needs to function properly and efficiently.

- Beetroot : Prevents cancer
- Carrots : Great way of protecting the skin from the sun
- Celery : Aids digestion, increases weight loss
- Ginger Root: Has anti-inflammatory effects
- Lime : It balances and maintains the pH level of the body
- Pepper: Supports Weight loss
- Spinach : Maintains muscle and nerve function

Ingredients:

- Beetroot - 170g
- Carrots - 210g

- Celery - 2 stalks, 125g

- Ginger Root - 1 thumb 20g

- Lime - 1/2 fruit 30g

- Pepper (jalapeno) - 1 pepper 10g

- Spinach - 2 cups 60g

How to prepare:

- **Wash all the ingredients. Peel if necessary.**

- **Juice them all together for a great drink.**

Total calories: 107

Vitamins: Vitamin A 1457µg, Vitamin C 48.4mg, Vitamin B-6 0.507mg, Vitamin E 2.49mg, Vitamin K 241.1µg, Calcium 155mg, Iron 3.01mg

Minerals: Copper 0.301mg, Magnesium 96mg, Phosphorus 151mg, Selenium 2µg, Zinc 1.21mg

32. Weight Fighter

"Weight Fighter" will make a difference for sure in your fight to get rid of fat, if it's consumed just a few times per week. These fruits and vegetables have a lot to offer because of the greens and roots it has. Beet greens are the leaves that come with the beet, they have a high concentration of vitamins when washed and blended into your juice.

- Apple: Because of the pectin, helps lose weight

- Beet Greens: They boost your stamina and fight inflammation

- Beetroot: Has anti-cancer effects

- Carrots: Improve vision and have an anti-aging effect

- Celery: Aids digestion because of the high water content combined with insoluble fiber

- Ginger root: Has a painkiller effect

Ingredients:

- Apple - 1 large 220g

- Beet Greens (optional) - 3 leaves 95g

- Beetroot - 1 beet 175g

- Carrots - 4 medium 240g
- Celery - 1 stalk, large 60g
- Ginger Root - 1/2 thumb 10g

How to prepare:

- **Wash all the ingredients. Peel if necessary.**
- **Juice them all together for a great drink.**

Total calories: 157

Vitamins: Vitamin A 1645µg, Vitamin C 45.1mg, Vitamin B-6 0.4mg, Vitamin E 2.59mg, Vitamin K 307.1µg, Calcium 181mg, Iron 3.51mg

Minerals: Copper 0.371mg, Magnesium 109mg, Phosphorus 162mg, Selenium 1.8µg, Zinc 1.21mg

33. Morning Breakfast

There is nothing more refreshing than an energy drink in the morning. By trying it on a daily basis, you increase your stamina and weight loss much faster than if you take it once a month. That is because of the high content of fiber and nutrients. "Morning Breakfast" is also very low in calories, and contains turmeric root which is a very good anti-inflammatory, and one of nature's great healers.

- Apple: Contains natural laxative
- Carrot: Do wonders for boosting the immune system
- Celery: Calms the nerve because of high calcium content
- Ginger root: Lowers the LDL cholesterol
- Lemon: Great for health problems because it contains potassium
- Pears: Have anti-oxidants that help prevent high blood pressure
- Turmeric root: Has powerful anti-inflammatory effects

Ingredients:

- Apples - 2 medium 360g

- Carrots - 3 medium 180g

- Celery - 3 stalks, large 190g

- Ginger Root - 1 thumb 22g

- Lemons (peeled) - 2 fruits 165g

- Pears - 2 medium 355g

- Turmeric Root - 6 thumbs 140g

How to prepare:

- **Wash all the ingredients. Peel if necessary.**

- **Juice them all together for a great drink.**

Total calories: 364

Vitamins: Vitamin A 1107µg, Vitamin C 283.1mg, Vitamin B-6 1.025mg, Vitamin E 2mg, Vitamin K 73.6µg, Calcium 191mg, Iron 3.41mg

Minerals: Copper 0.743mg, Magnesium 115mg, Phosphorus 212mg, Selenium 1.5µg, Zinc 1.35mg

34. Start Healthy

Sweet potatoes are full of potassium and calcium which are important for everyone, no matter what your lifestyle. "Start Healthy" is rich in vitamins and minerals. Try this drink about 30-60 minutes before eating, to allow your body to absorb all the nutrients from fruits and vegetables first.

- Apples: Reduce risk of cancer
- Beetroots: Cleanse the colon and strengthen the liver
- Carrot: Beta-carotene lowers risk of muscular degeneration
- Orange: Stimulates white cells to fight infection
- Pepper: Has antioxidant and antibacterial effects
- Sweet Potato: Helps the immune system get stronger

Ingredients:

- Apples (golden delicious) - 2 medium 360g
- Beetroots - 2 beets 160g
- Carrot - 1 large 70g
- Orange (optional) - 1 fruit 135g
- Pepper (sweet red) - 1 medium 115g

- Sweet Potato – 130g

How to prepare:

- **Wash all the ingredients. Peel if necessary.**
- **Juice them all together for a great drink.**

Total calories: 250

Vitamins: Vitamin A 1211µg, Vitamin C 177.5mg, Vitamin B-6 0.735mg, Vitamin E 2.51mg, Vitamin K 18.1µg, Calcium 118mg, Iron 2.31mg

Minerals: Copper 0.35mg, Magnesium 85mg, Phosphorus 167mg, Selenium 1.8µg, Zinc 1.15mg

35. Natural Mix

Juices have always been a delicious drink, but they are more than just that, they are a fountain of health and, if made properly with the right ingredients, they can provide all the vitamins your body needs. This is a great juice recipe that has weight loss effects and helps the immune system build up. You should drink it in the morning or in the evening after dinner. Let's see what great effects it will have on your own body.

- Apple: Contains boron, for bones strength

- Celery: Has nutrients that protect the eyes and prevent age-related degeneration of vision

- Cucumber: Great source of silicon that improves health of the skin

- Dandelion Greens: help reduce stress and reduce cancer

- Kale: Provides a large nutritional punch with few calorie count

- Lemon: Helps increase weight loss

Ingredients:

- Apples - 2 medium 360g

- Celery - 2 stalks, medium 80g
- Cucumber - 1/2 cucumber 150g
- Dandelion Greens - 1 cup, chopped 55g
- Kale - 3 leaves 105g
- Lemon - 1/2 fruit 42g

How to prepare:

- **Wash all the ingredients. Peel if necessary.**
- **Juice them all together for a great drink.**

Total calories: 165

Vitamins: Vitamin A 581µg, Vitamin C 133.2mg, Vitamin B-6 0.504mg, Vitamin E 2mg, Vitamin K 854µg, Calcium 238mg, Iron 3.13mg

Minerals: Copper 1.29mg, Magnesium 81mg, Phosphorus 163mg, Selenium 1.4µg, Zinc 0.95mg

36. Surprise Juice

Weight loss has always been associated with juice recipes, because they have few calories, and the nutrients get absorbed faster by your body. It should be consumed within 30-60 minutes before a meal, and the effects should be felt only after a week or so. Here are some great benefits of this juice that for sure will improve your health condition.

- Apple: Protects brain cells from free radical damage

- Carrot: Consumption of beta-carotene has been linked to reduce risk of several cancers

- Cilantro: Reduces the amount of damaged fats in the cell membranes

- Collard Green: Rich in source of nutrients with anti-cancer properties

- Kale: Contains sulforaphane that helps support a healthy immune system

- Pepper: Has antioxidant abilities so it can neutralize free radicals in the body

Ingredients:

- Apple - 1 medium 180g

- Carrots - 3 medium 180g

- Cilantro - 1 handful 35g

- Collard Greens - 1 cup, chopped 35g

- Kale - 4 leaves (8-12") 140g

- Pepper (sweet red) - 1 medium 115g

How to prepare:

- **Wash all the ingredients. Peel if necessary.**

- **Juice them all together for a great drink.**

Total calories: 158

Vitamins: Vitamin A 1832µg, Vitamin C 252.1mg, Vitamin B-6 0.812mg, Vitamin E 3.52mg, Vitamin K 898.1µg, Calcium 275mg, Iron 2.86mg

Minerals: Copper 1.61mg, Magnesium 90mg, Phosphorus 187mg, Selenium 1.6µg, Zinc 1.28mg

37. Broccoli Combo

"Broccoli Combo" is simple to prepare, you should drink it in the morning so you can charge yourself with energy for the rest of the day. If you can have it every two days, it will be even more beneficial. It has a high percentage of vitamin C that will make your immune system stronger and give you strength to fight any health problems.

- **Broccoli :** Is high on iron, which is an important nutrient to ensure energy levels stay high

- **Cabbage:** Helps detoxify the body and keeps blood pressure from getting high

- **Kale:** Helps in proper functioning of insulin and regulates blood sugar

Ingredients:

- Broccoli - 1 stalk 150g

- Cabbage - 1/2 head, medium 450g

- Kale - 4 leaves (8-12") 140g

How to prepare:

- **Wash all the ingredients. Peel if necessary.**

- **Juice them all together for a great drink.**

Total calories: 117

Vitamins: Vitamin A 536µg, Vitamin C 328.1mg, Vitamin B-6 0.841mg, Vitamin E 1mg, Vitamin K 1038.6µg, Calcium 321mg, Iron 3.68mg

Minerals: Copper 1.571mg, Magnesium 102mg, Phosphorus 241mg, Selenium 4.3µg, Zinc 1.41mg

38. Tropical Ginger

If you plan on having a healthy diet and losing some weight, then this juice recipe should be on the menu as well. "Tropical Ginger" is full of vitamins and nutrients that will not only benefit your body, but will also increase your energy levels throughout the day. For this recipe you will need the listed ingredients and you should enjoy the juice in the evening.

- Ginger Root: Prevents cancerous tumor growth, and can help knock out a fever

- Kale: Is a rich source of organosulfur compounds that fight many cancers

- Mango: Contains enzymes that help in breaking down protein

- Orange: Contains hesperidin that lowers high blood pressure

- Pineapple: Decreases risk of progression of age-related muscular degeneration

Ingredients:

- Ginger Root - 1/2 thumb 10g

- Kale - 4 leaves (8-12") 140g

- Mango - 1 fruit without refuse 335g
- Orange - 1 small 95g
- Pineapple - 1 cup, chunks 165g

How to prepare:

- **Wash all the ingredients. Peel if necessary.**
- **Juice them all together for a great drink.**

Total calories: 231

Vitamins: Vitamin A 625µg, Vitamin C 294.2mg, Vitamin B-6 0.725mg, Vitamin E 2.24mg, Vitamin K 701.2µg, Calcium 215mg, Iron 2.25mg

Minerals: Copper 1.904mg, Magnesium 93mg, Phosphorus 143mg, Selenium 2.5µg, Zinc 0.95mg

39. Lemon King

Juice recipes are a healthy and modern way of staying fit to making sure your body gets all the important nutrients, minerals and vitamins it needs. It is best to have this juice in the morning, or you can also replace a daily snack with it. If you drink this juice on a daily basis you will feel the effects in your body and in your mind as well.

- Apple: Reduces cholesterol and decreases risk of diabetes

- Celery: Regulates the body's alkaline balance

- Kale: Helps support a healthy immune system and has anti-cancer properties

- Lemon: prevents problems related to skin

- Spinach: Great to lower blood pressure, and cleans out the system by removing accumulated wastes

Ingredients:

- Apples (granny smith) - 4 medium 725g

- Celery - 3 stalks, large 190g

- Kale - 2 leaves (8-12") 70g

- Lemon (peeled) - 1 fruit 58g

- Spinach - 4 cups 120g

How to prepare:

- **Wash all the ingredients. Peal if necessary.**
- **Juice them all together for a great drink.**

Total calories: 254

Vitamins: Vitamin A 679µg, Vitamin C 131.4mg, Vitamin B-6 0.627mg, Vitamin E 3.03mg, Vitamin K 801.2µg, Calcium 251mg, Iron 4.11mg

Minerals: Copper 1.041mg, Magnesium 131mg, Phosphorus 180mg, Selenium 2µg, Zinc 1.10mg

40. Huge Mix

One of the best methods to lose weight and drop fat is by starting the day off with this delicious juice. Bell peppers help increase our body's metabolism by lowering triglycerides which are stored in our body, and this helps burn calories more effectively. Here are other benefits from this juice recipe:

- Cayenne Pepper : Blocks transmission of pain, so it can help relieve the pain to a certain degree

- Celery : Reduces high blood pressure

- Cilantro: Is very low in calories and contains no cholesterol

- Garlic : Reduces blood triglycerides and reduces arterial plaque formation

- Onion : For centuries, onions have been used to reduce inflammation and heal infections

- Tomato : Has anti-oxidant properties and improves the digestive function

Ingredients:

- Cayenne Pepper (spice) 0.20g

- Celery - 1 stalk, large 63g

- Cilantro - 1 handful 35g

- Garlic - 1 clove 3g

- Onion (spring/scallion) - 1 medium 14g

- Pepper (sweet green) - 1 medium 115g

- Salt (himalayan) - 1 dash 0.2g

- Tomato - 1 cup cherry tomatoes 145g

How to prepare:

- **Wash all the ingredients. Peel if necessary.**

- **Juice them all together for a great drink.**

Total calories: 35

Vitamins: Vitamin A 156µg, Vitamin C 91.5mg, Vitamin B-6 0.370mg, Vitamin E 1.65mg, Vitamin K 122.2µg, Calcium 63mg, Iron 1.25mg

Minerals: Copper 0.200mg, Magnesium 33mg, Phosphorus 70mg, Selenium 0.7µg, Zinc 0.52mg

41. Granny Juice

If you are a juice lover, here is a great recipe for you. It will help improve your body's metabolism and increase weight loss. It is best to be served in the morning or within 30 to 60 minutes before having a meal or you can easily replace a snack with it. This juice has a high content of potassium and phosphorous, which helps release the symptoms of stress. So if you are having a bad day, you can always relax and enjoy this drink, it will help. Here are some other great effects of this recipe:

- Apple: Great source of fiber without too many calories

- Carrot: Very rich in vitamin A, good for improving eyesight

- Cucumber: Relieves bad breath and rehydrates body

- Grapes: Reduce cells ability to store fat by about 130 percent, significantly assisting in weight loss

- Pepper: Stimulates white cells to fight infection, naturally building a good immune system

- Spinach: High alkalinity properties make it perfect choice for people suffering inflammatory ailments, like osteoarthritis

- Tomato: Improves heart health by helping lower blood pressure

Ingredients:

- Apples (green) - 2 medium 355g
- Carrots - 3 medium 180g
- Cucumber - 1 cucumber 300g
- Grapes (green) - 15 grapes 90g
- Pepper (sweet green) - 1 medium 115g
- Spinach - 2 cups 60g
- Tomato - 1 medium whole 115g

How to prepare:

- **Wash all the ingredients. Peel if necessary.**
- **Juice them all together for a great drink.**

Total calories: 221

Vitamins: Vitamin A 1325µg, Vitamin C 114.2mg, Vitamin B-6 0.701mg, Vitamin E 2.79mg, Vitamin K 270.1µg, Calcium 171mg, Iron 2.9mg

Minerals: Copper 0.429mg, Magnesium 112mg, Phosphorus 185mg, Selenium 1.1mg, Zinc 1.31mg

42. Mineral Fountain

No matter what kind of lifestyle you have, you should make time for a healthy juice that can be an excellent source of minerals and vitamins. If you want to lose weight, improve your health, or just feel better, a natural juice can do that for you. It's a true friend when it comes down to improving the way your body looks, works and feels, and the outcome will definitely be a positive one. Here are the benefits of this juice recipe.

- Apple: One apple per day reduces risk of breast cancer by 16 percent

- Beetroot: Very healing for liver toxicity or bile ailments such as food poisoning, hepatitis

- Ginger Root: Reduces inflammation and inhibits replication of the herpes simplex virus

- Lemon: Adding lemon juice will help increase weight loss

- Pineapple: Helps combat the formation of free radicals known to cause cancer

Ingredients:

- Apple - 1 medium 180g

- Beetroot (golden) - 1 beet 80g

- Ginger Root - 1 thumb 24g

- Lemon - 1/2 fruit 29g

- Pineapple - 2 slices 332g

- Pumpkin Pie Spice (a dash) - 1/4 tsp 0.42g

How to prepare:

- **Wash all the ingredients. Peel if necessary.**

- **Juice them all together for a great drink.**

Total calories: 179

Vitamins: Vitamin A 11µg, Vitamin C 121.4mg, Vitamin B-6 0.385mg, Vitamin E 0.35mg, Vitamin K 4.5µg, Calcium 55mg, Iron 1.53mg

Minerals: Copper 0.36mg, Magnesium 56mg, Phosphorus 64mg, Selenium 0.8µg, Zinc 0.60mg

43. Health Friend

Here is a great and easy to make juice recipe that will give you incredible weight loss results and helping you get all the necessary nutrients your body needs. It's a great way to saving time and will maximize your day. You can easily replace an unhealthy snack with this juice. Here are the effects from this juice:

- Asparagus: Contains potassium that is known for reducing fat, and it's also low in natural sodium and has no cholesterol, which helps when trying to lose weight

- Celery: Has high antioxidant content, and has an antibacterial effect against Salmonella

- Cilantro: Is a natural water purifier, and a vital nutrient that is required for formation and maintenance of strong bones

Ingredients:

- Asparagus - 6 spears, medium 95g
- Celery - 3 stalks, large 185g
- Cilantro - 1 handful 32g

How to prepare:

- **Wash all the ingredients. Peel if necessary.**

- **Juice them all together for a great drink.**

Total calories: 20

Vitamins: Vitamin A 131µg, Vitamin C 14.2mg, Vitamin B-6 0.185mg, Vitamin E 1.63mg, Vitamin K 139.1µg, Calcium 84mg, Iron 2.09mg

Minerals: Copper 0.218mg, Magnesium 28mg, Phosphorus 75mg, Selenium 2.1µg, Zinc 0.63mg

44. Sweet Juice

You will have fun making this juice recipe, it's easy to prepare and all the ingredients are delightful. So let's get started, try to serve this juice at least 30 to 60 minutes before eating your next meal. "Sweet Juice" is a great way to accelerate weight loss and improve your health at the same time. If you are ready, let's review some of the benefits that will come from this recipe.

- **Beetroot:** High in carbohydrates which means it is a great instant energy source, and useful in helping metabolize fat

- **Carrot:** Has a cleaning action on the liver and lowers the cholesterol levels

- **Sweet Potato:** Contains anti-inflammatory nutrients

Ingredients:

- Beetroot - 1 beet 80g

- Carrots - 3 medium 181g

- Sweet Potato - 1/2 63g

How to prepare:

- **Wash all the ingredients. Peel if necessary.**

- **Juice them all together for a great drink.**

Total calories: 85

Vitamins: Vitamin A 1386µg, Vitamin C 11.2mg, Vitamin B-6 0.30mg, Vitamin E 0.92mg, Vitamin K 17.4µg, Calcium 63mg, Iron 1.10mg

Minerals: Copper 0.165mg, Magnesium 39mg, Phosphorus 87mg, Selenium 0.7µg, Zinc 0.61mg

45. Pure Life

Bring this healthy juice recipe into your life, the effects will change your weight problems in a positive way and make your body stronger. You can drink it any time of the day; just make sure you do it 30 to 60 minutes before having a meal. Ok, so let's see now what this juice has to offer for you.

- Bitter Melon: Contains a chemical that acts like insulin to help reduce blood sugar levels

- Grapefruit: Works as an excellent appetite suppressant and also beneficial in the treatment of fatigue

- Lemon: Assists in curing respiratory problems, and helps increasing weight loss

Ingredients:

- Bitter Melon - 1 bitter melon 120g

- Grapefruit - 1/2 large 165g

- Lemon (with peel) - 1 fruit 80g

How to prepare:

- **Wash all the ingredients. Peel if necessary.**

- **Juice them all together for a great drink.**

Total calories: 45

Vitamins: Vitamin A 73µg, Vitamin C 142mg, Vitamin B-6 0.131mg, Vitamin E 0.23mg, Folate 80µg, Calcium 45mg, Iron 0.81mg

Minerals: Copper 0.102mg, Magnesium 27mg, Phosphorus 43mg, Selenium 0.7µg, Zinc 0.80mg

46. Vitamin Time

We all want to be healthy, but most of the time we forget that we have to act responsibly to do this. Juice recipes are an excellent way to solve this problem. A couple of minutes a day and you get a big flow of vitamins and minerals. "Vitamin Time" fits the description and let's see what it has to offer.

- Apple: Contains pectin that lowers cholesterol
- Carrot: Eliminates excess fluids from the body and reduces stroke risk
- Ginger Root: Helps digesting fatty foods and breaks down proteins, helping in reducing weight
- Lemon: Inhibits the development of cancer, and increases weight loss

Ingredients:

- Apple - 1 medium 180g
- Carrots - 8 medium 485g
- Ginger Root - 1 thumb 22g
- Lemon - 1 fruit 82g

How to prepare:

- **Wash all the ingredients. Peel if necessary.**

- **Juice them all together for a great drink.**

Total calories: 165

Vitamins: Vitamin A 2851µg, Vitamin C 56mg, Vitamin B-6 0.589mg, Vitamin E 2.50mg, Vitamin K 46.8µg, Calcium 132mg, Iron 1.61mg

Minerals: Copper 0.242mg, Magnesium 58mg, Phosphorus 145mg, Selenium 0.6µg, Zinc 0.94mg

47. Tasty ABC

This juice recipe is best to be served in the morning because it is a great way to give your body an energy boost, and it will also keep your mind focused and active for the rest of the day. If you were looking for something to help you with the benefits mentioned above, or just looking for that recipe that helps reducing fat, you should try this one. Here are some other benefits it has to offer.

- Apple: Boosts the immune system and helps detoxify your liver

- Beetroot: Lowers blood pressure, very rich in fiber and is a great source of betaine, a nutrient that helps protects cells

- Carrots: Prevent heart disease and cleanse the body

Ingredients:

- Apple - 1 medium 180g

- Beet Root - 1 beet 80g

- Carrots - 2 large 141g

How to prepare:

- **Wash all the ingredients. Peel if necessary.**

- **Juice them all together for a great drink.**

Total calories: 95

Vitamins: Vitamin A 837μg. Vitamin C 13.5mg, Vitamin B-6 0.21mg, Vitamin E 0.88mg, Vitamin K 16.1μg, Calcium 49mg, Iron 0.90mg

Minerals: Copper 0.121mg, Magnesium 31mg, Phosphorus 71mg, Selenium 0.4μg, Zinc 0.47mg

48. Delight in Three

"Delight in Three" is a simple juice recipe that can be served to the entire family, just make sure you do it 30 to 60 minutes before having a meal. Feel free to try it and see the results; it's going to bring only positive things into your life, for your health and the way your body look. Let's see how to prepare it and what it will provide.

- Apple: Increases bone density, boosts the immune system and reduces cholesterol

- Beetroot: Regenerates and reactivates the red blood cells and supplies fresh oxygen to the body

- Sweet Potato: Plays an important role in our energy levels, moods, heart, nerves, skin, and teeth.

Ingredients:

- Apples - 2 medium 360g

- Beet Root - 1 beet 80g

- Sweet Potato - 135g

How to prepare:

- **Wash all the ingredients. Peel if necessary.**

- **Juice them all together for a great drink.**

Total calories: 175

Vitamins: Vitamin A 643µg, Vitamin C 16.5mg, Vitamin B-6 0.331mg, Vitamin E 0.71mg, Vitamin K 7.3µg, Calcium 51mg, Iron 1.31mg

Minerals: Copper 0.247mg, Magnesium 48mg, Phosphorus 92mg, Selenium 0.8µg, Zinc 0.56mg

49. Evening Flavor

No more excuses when it comes to losing weight. "Evening Flavor" is a great juice recipe that's perfect for the job. You should drink it in the morning to get the most of it for the rest of the day. It won't take more than 5 minutes to prepare, and for those 5 minutes you will get awesome results! Check out what is waiting for you.

- Beetroot:
- Carrot:
- Celery:
- Cucumber:
- Pear:
- Ginger Root:

Ingredients:

- Beetroot (golden) - 1 beet 80g
- Carrots - 3 large 215g
- Celery - 4 stalks, large 255g
- Cucumber - 1/2 cucumber 150g
- Ginger Root - 1/2 thumb 11g

- Pear (bosc) - 1 medium 174g

How to prepare:

- **Wash all the ingredients. Peel if necessary.**
- **Juice them all together for a great drink.**

Total calories: 147

Vitamins: Vitamin A 1304µg, Vitamin C 25mg, Vitamin B-6 0.462mg, Vitamin E 1.66mg, Vitamin K 1.82mg, Calcium 158mg, Iron 1.73mg

Minerals: Copper 0.334mg, Magnesium 75mg, Phosphorus 161mg, Selenium 1.7µg, Zinc 1.15mg

50. Vegetable Time

Here is a great juice recipe that you must try. If you are on a diet or want to have a healthier body, it will help. It's easy to prepare and you should drink it in the morning as an extra snack. The ingredients are high on important nutrients and very low on calories, so it will help you accelerate your progress. Let's see what benefits await you with this recipe.

- **Beetroots:** They fight inflammation and lower your blood pressure
- **Carrots:** Great source of beta-carotene that reduces risk of cancer
- **Celery:** Reduces cholesterol and regulates your alkaline balance
- **Parsley:** Excellent blood purifier and builder
- **Pepper:** Has antibacterial and antioxidant effects
- **Radishes:** Great way to satisfy hunger and keep a low caloric intake
- **Tomatoes:** The fiber, potassium, vitamin C and choline content in tomatoes all support heart health

Ingredients:

- Beetroot - 1 beet 81g
- Carrots - 2 medium 121g
- Celery - 2 stalks, large 125g
- Parsley - 4 handful 160g
- Pepper (jalapeno) (seeds/ribs removed) - 1 pepper 13g
- Radishes - 12 medium 50g
- Tomatoes - 4 plum tomatoes 246g

How to prepare:

- **Wash all the ingredients. Peel if necessary.**
- **Juice them all together for a great drink.**

Total calories: 100

Vitamins: Vitamin A 1273µg, Vitamin C 200.4mg, Vitamin B-6 0.51mg, Vitamin E 2.92mg, Vitamin K 1890.3µg, Calcium 254mg, Iron 8.45mg

Minerals: Copper 0.403mg, Magnesium 113mg, Phosphorus 190mg, Selenium 1.1µg, Zinc 2.11mg

OTHER GREAT TITLES BY THIS AUTHOR

Advanced Mental Toughness Training for Bodybuilders

Using Visualization to Push Yourself to the Limit

By

Joseph Correa

Certified Sports Nutritionist

Becoming Mentally Tougher in Bodybuilding by Using Meditation

Reach Your Potential by Controlling Your Inner Thoughts

By

Joseph Correa

Certified Sports Nutritionist

www.ingramcontent.com/pod-product-compliance
Lightning Source LLC
Chambersburg PA
CBHW071742080526
44588CB00013B/2129